"*SAHARA* is a stellar collection—comprehensive, varied, challenging and reassuring. It is sensitive to the textures and tonalities replete in everyday objects and events, at the same time as imbibing them with an importance they would never have outside the poetic text. Ahmed Elbeshlawy's variety of voices deftly exploits different registers throughout, and whilst they are accessible, they imbibe the simplest of his subjects with a depth and an open, intuitive suggestibility. Though seemingly straightforward, he ironically reveals that little in this world is dismissible and unimportant. Herein lies the heart of the architecture of and the richness therein of *SAHARA*."

—Prof. George Watt, author & poet

"Elbeshlawy's poetic voice is eclectic. *SAHARA* is at once a love saga, a work of philosophy, and a cultural critique. Those Hong Kong-Egypt-based poems are not only written with great passion but are also the product of an interdisciplinary mind that shifts sharply - and delightfully - between the urban, the literary, the social, and the psychoanalytic."

—Cecilia Kak, Programme Director, English Studies,
        HKU School of Professional and Continuing Education

I first encountered Ahmed Elbeshlawy as a reader in 'Poetry Outloud' Hong Kong's longest running spoken-word open mic. He struck me then as confident, open minded and willing to tackle personal and sensitive topics in his work. This analysis has only been reinforced by reading this latest collection of Poetry, *SAHARA*. In the introduction to this collection he outlines the many facets of meaning related to the Sahara Desert and the linguistic connections and connotations of the name itself. It is an apt title for this collection which contains the facets of his own life, thoughts and experience through many years in Hong Kong, as an exile from Egypt, the land of his birth. He has the insider's knowledge of the city but the outsider's perspective. Many of the poems are explicitly located in the geographical location of Hong Kong (Tsing Yi), whereas others are located in the mind and or the emotions of the poet, often drawing the comparisons between imagined love and the prosaic reality of relationships. This delicious cynicism is often on display in other poems, for example in 'Incredible'. There are hints of Rumi in some of the pieces; 'Sinai' evokes the fantasy of a new Rumi poem; perhaps titled 'In Hong Kong Dreaming of Cairo'! There are also elements of Bukowski in the celebration of strong drink. Despite these real or imagined influences Elbeshlawy's work explicitly contains his own voice and style. He doesn't shy away from criticism of religion and the inherent hypocrisy in many of it's practitioners (A Dream, A Better Moslem). Overall *SAHARA* provides a miscellany of poems that reward the reading and rereading of them.

—DAVID MCKIRDY, car mechanic, poet, author, editor

Dr. Ahmed Elbeshlawy is a noted teacher of comparative literature in Hong Kong where he has lived since 1995. A cosmopolitan, fluent in a number of languages, he teaches and writes about literature ranging from Donne to Akhmatova, Yeats to Cavafy. A previous book of poetry, *Savage Charm*, was largely concerned with his perceptions of the city after more than a quarter of a century in Hong Kong. *Sahara* is more broad-ranging in its themes and concerns. He explores the erotics of poetry and the poetry of love ("Forbid black, the colour of death/ from becoming/ the colour of underwear" - p.74). Like Li Bai, the poetic imbiber, he celebrates the ink and drink link, of wine and poetry (*The Connection* - p.20). Ahmed knows his *Qur'an*. He celebrates the landscape of the Middle East – "stars over the Sinai desert". Yet he is not afraid to challenge "those scared of a free mind", those such as the "beards of Kabul/putting millions of women back/in the dark" (p.79) or the horror of a woman hanged and stoned to death while the event is recorded by children on their mobile phones (*A Dream* - p. 21). Opposed to those who live in a "cultural cocoon" are those who venture out (p. 49), who question received opinions and preconceptions (*The Name* - p.13). He evokes poignant memories and recollections, of, for instance, young love - what was left unsaid and what is now regretted. A central concern is with the careful and accurate use of English in an age of "like, like, likeness" (*Incredible* - p. 40). He gives a fascinating exposition of how the word *Sahara* changes meaning with the addition of diacritics or a focus on the fricative 'h': from magic, to sleeplessness, to watching the moon, to being in love; an etymology that is an entire cultural history of thoughts and feelings. Throughout the collection, there are paeans of praise for the efficacy of poetry, for its importance, especially in times when it is reviled or deemed useless. Those who share his conviction should read this volume.

—Dr. Peter Kennedy, Honorary Associate Professor, HKU

"Some real beauty here. Presence, poise and poetry. There is the welcome alerting crispness of morning desert dew across the collection; with a variety of powerfully sustaining tastes in the life-creating liquid too."

—Dr. Andrew Barker, poet

SAHARA

SAHARA

AHMED ELBESHLAWY

Foreword by Paola Caronni

RESOURCE *Publications* · Eugene, Oregon

SAHARA

Resource Publications
An Imprint of Wipf and Stock Publishers
199 W. 8th Ave., Suite 3
Eugene, OR 97401

www.wipfandstock.com

PAPERBACK ISBN: 978-1-6667-7267-8
HARDCOVER ISBN: 978-1-6667-7268-5
EBOOK ISBN: 978-1-6667-7270-8

R

Contents

Contents

CONTENTS

Foreword

IN THE INTRIGUING AUTHOR'S introduction to *SAHARA*, Ahmed Elbeshlawy explains the many interpretations of the word 'Sahara', which emerge once we start playing with its etymology, phonology, and semantics. This is an apt invitation to explore the vastness of the desert, wandering like Bedouins and Tuaregs across the dunes to see what is to be found in this vastity, while our gaze gets lost in a seemingly immutable landscape. This is the poet's *Sahara* tough, and the landscape keeps changing.

There is moon gazing. There is suffering for unrequited love. There are white nights accompanied by too much red wine (a source of poetry inspiration, it appears). There are recollections of sensual and sexual pleasures. There is the beauty of Nature, and the realisation that in front of its wonders, we're simply too small and insignificant, even as we leave Sahara and we move to Sinai 'The cold night, though quiet,//Had the loudest voice...how to bring//The stars down to earth (*"Sinai"*).

The voice accompanying us as we tread the fine sand is sometimes angry about the misinterpretation of religion and Islam, and also about religious indoctrination in the (so-called) name of God. Other times it's nostalgic, and very often ironic and sarcastic, like in *"A Feminist Bride"*. The speaker remembers past lovers – and frequently goes back to the woman who never became one of them – feeling inadequate, and powerless.

As Rumi wrote in *"The sunrise Ruby"*: 'There's nothing left of me. I'm like a ruby held up to the sunrise. It is still a stone, or a world made of redness?' There is more than redness here. *SA-HARA* is a long love song that subsumes its own poetic world as if seen through a prism, which 'distorts// Slants, or colors whatever// Is observed through it' *("Prism")*. Rumi often comes to mind when the poet tells us stories and anecdotes, like in *"Exile"*, where poetry seems to be the only refuge: 'Now old, bent, and wanting nothing// But his undoing, he builds edifices of poetic ruin,//Made out of his raging and rambling way of living,//To shout his pain out loud'.

Indeed, relevant protagonists of *SAHARA* are the act of making poetry, and the freedom of writing it. *SAHARA* is thus a testament to loving and writing, two actions that commingle and sometimes compete to get priority. As the speaker feels lost, salvation comes through the gates of memories that take him back to the unreciprocated or lost love, and through the act of writing: 'nothing can save a sinner//From the sin of writing//Other than the sin of falling//In love for no good reason.' (*"Let them Come"*).

If it is the act of writing that makes a man a real poet 'When writing becomes//More enjoyable//Than being with a beautiful// Woman in bed,//You're definitely a poet.' (*"Being a Poet"*), man is also weak, and cannot live on poetry only. In all his sincerity, the speaker tells his woman 'Don't you think it is about time//We put aside dear poetry//And try to start heading somewhere//South far from the heads and letting//The bodies talk instead all night?' (*"Poetic Messages"*).

Ultimately, we're human. And we sympathise with the speaker – and the poet – for being so sincere and vulnerable, allowing us to enjoy every verse of this lush poetry collection, and retain it for a long time. By the time we finish reading the last page, we leave the shimmering desert behind and look at things with brand-new eyes.

Paola Caronni,
author of the poetry collection *Uncharted Waters*,
winner of the Proverse Prize 2020

Acknowledgements

I AM GRATEFUL TO Paola Caronni for her close reading of the poems of *SAHARA* and the insightful foreword that she wrote to this collection. I would also like to thank George Watt, David McKirdy, Andrew Barker, Peter Kennedy, and Cecilia Kak for reading *SAHARA* and writing advance comments on the work.

Four poems from *SAHARA*, namely, "Blanchot", "Sandy Eyes", "Sinai", and "The Onslaught of Sameness" appeared before in Proverse Hong Kong's anthology *Mingled Voices 7*. My thanks go to Dr. Verner Bickley and Dr. Gillian Bickley for that.

Finally yet importantly, I would like to thank my favourite artist, Ms. Malak Elbeshlawy, for designing the front cover image of *SAHARA*.

Author's Introduction

SAHARA IS THE LARGEST hot desert in the world. Ancient Egyptians called it "deshret" (red land). The name "Sahara" is derived from the Arabic word for desert in the feminine irregular form. The dominant extra-low central vowel in it together with the Semitic glottal strong "h" signify unfathomable vastness, emptiness, and dryness. Without the final "a", the romanized word becomes "sahar", which means "predawn" in Arabic. The Qur'an recounts how God destroyed the people of Lot by unleashing upon them a storm of stones made of baked clay, delivering only Lot's family (the believers) before dawn (at sahar), in a Qur'anic Sura entitled "Al-Qamar" (The Moon). A slight change in the diacritics of the Arabic word "sahar", without changing any letters, makes it "sehr" (magic), while changing the Semitic glottal "h" to a voiceless fricative "h" changes the meaning of the word to "staying awake at night" or "sleeplessness" which, in the tradition and literary imagination of the people of the Sahara, is connected to ideas of watching the moon, being in love, suffering unrequited love, or writing in the quiet of the night. All of this is intrinsically mixed together in this collection.

Prism

A prism,
According to *Merriam-Webster*,
Is a "medium that distorts,
Slants, or colors whatever
Is observed through it".

If I am
To give one long-lasting lecture
On what desire contorts,
I'd say your feel and figure –
Both are bent by it.

A Naked Lunatic on the Highway

How many more are there
In that vast desert?
I tend to think that the number
Is underestimated.
How many, stark naked,
sleep at night exposed
To the elements?
How frequently do they venture
Going out on the highway –
Oblivious to the glass and steel
Rushing by menacingly
Close to their fragile flesh?
How many had previous lives
In different worlds?
How many went from snugging
With warm bodies to trembling
Under torn and worn-out blankets?
How many of them lost their minds
Over certain words?
How many of them are poets?

Tsing Yi

There's too much urbanization
And too much boredom;
Too many people and too many trains
In and out of the station;
There are too many vehicles
And too many tall buildings;
Too many malls and bright lights;
Too many sounds in muted crowdedness -
Just too much for our Tsing Yi.

Where are the pier and the boats?
Where are the young boys
And girls drinking beer at night
And shouting over who knows what?
Where are the dusty roads?
Where is the fenceless walk by the sea?
Where are the rocks and the fishing lines?
Where is the bustling emptiness?
Where are we? Where are we?

Daddy

The nurse handed me the scissors.
I cut the umbilical cord –
Which was much harder than I thought.
They washed the little big-headed
Red piece of flesh in a small sink,
Dried it softly with cotton cloth,
Dipped one foot in some bluish ink,
Printed it firmly on a card,
Amid the blaring cries of one
Who seemed to be torn away from sweet home.

"O, Congratulations, Daddy!",
One of the helping nurses yelled,
"It's a lovely baby girl, and,
She's two-point-eighty-three kg".
She handed her over to me
Like she was washing her hands clean
Of some responsibility –
Like she wanted nothing to do
With yet another crime that has
Been committed against humanity.

"Thank you", I mumbled, receiving
The delivery with great joy,
But also, with a sort of twinge.
It was the sur-reality
Of it that irked me – of "daddy",
Being said so casually,
Ignoring one key question: How
Does sleeping with a woman who
Next conceives a two-point-eighty-
Three kg baby make me a father?

Inspired by Paola Caronni's "Ahmed's Chimera"
from her Proverse Prize winning collection *Uncharted Waters*

The Name

Ahmed,
My proper name,
My friend for life,
My double,
Let me count the ways
You are both bliss and trouble:

Ahmed the Muslim,
Ahmed the immigrant,
Ahmed the Islamist,
Ahmed the different,
Ahmed the terrorist,

Ahmed the scholar,
Ahmed the thinker,
Ahmed the teacher,
Ahmed the prophet,
Ahmed the poet,
Ahmed the hobbit.

Ahmed the zero level of humanity,
Ahmed the silent, the subaltern,
Ahmed the supine, the feminine,
Ahmed the unpredictable;
Ahmed who could be smiling
Amiably to his neighbours,
While hiding a bomb behind his back.

Ahmed the misrepresented,
Ahmed the underrepresented,
Ahmed the living dead,
Ahmed the mad,
Ahmed the sad,
Ahmed whose forehead
Is stuck to the praying mat.

Ahmed who's always in his place.
Ahmed who's always out of place.
Ahmed the in-between,
Ahmed who doesn't fit anywhere,
Ahmed who's loved and hated
Almost equally everywhere.

Ahmed
Is in the Qur'an 61:6.
Ahmed
Is all of this impossible mix.

Aesthetic Theory

Aesthetic theory,
My beautiful addiction,
Is the connection
Between the delicate bones
Of your Egyptian neck
And the spectacular speck
On your unforgettable round chin.

Aesthetic theory
Is simply the reflection
Of poetic sin
By such a plentiful pen,
Sketching the line of your back
With nothing but words that peck
On dreamy nipples that should have been.

Grammatical Mistake

I received your letter,
In which you describe me as
A tremendous lover,
However,
There's something wrong
In the grammar
Of what you wrote to me.

Well, I know that is not
The important point – to you.
But it does show
That the letter
Was written in haste.

You see? The sea of love neither
Pays attention to those who drown,
Nor cares about
Those who stay afloat.
Nothing, however, goes to waste.

The bodies of the dead
Keep coming with the waves;
They keep hitting the living
With flesh and bones
That have nothing to lose.

In any case,
You don't want the same corpse
Returning, each morning,
Because of some mistake
In grammar.

Gadamer himself would find it
Insufferable.

Tell you what,
Try to write me a perfect letter,
And I promise,
I will go away –
Forever.

A Poem from Underground

If I'm to write like Dostoevsky,
From underground –
And I know I can't because I'm not good enough –
I would at least give you
This piece of my mind:
I know I've always been quite blind
To what you think you require;
I know I've been bookish and boring,
And beastly on top of that in my
Depraved demands of your delicate frame;
I know I never treated you as a dame
Or as a princess from ancient Rome.
And I know that you wonder,
Everyday,
If life is worth spending
With such an aloof and selfish lover.
I know, my love, that you suffer
Under this roof which doesn't seem
To protect you from the scorching sun
That slashes our bodies
Every time I write a poem
For you, my love, for torturing
Your beloved body – again.
And yes, the poem is a crime,
And an abomination,
And a great sin.

Exile

Once upon a time,
A boy was banished from his beloved's heart,
So, he banished the whole town.
Feeling so angry about being axed without mercy,
He tiptoed tactically on titillating tits
Of tender souls that didn't see the stealth
Behind his strange silence, which
Was often broken by knackering knockoffs
Of borrowed bywords from different philosophers.

Not a boy anymore, and living in exile
In a foreign city far away by many a mile
From where his first love felled
His fervor for finer feelings,
The black beast of prey loved
And left green-leaved girls
With nothing but pellucid pearls
Running down their delicate velvety cheeks.

Near dead-drunk, he dreamt of daisies
That just sprung from long-lost faces,
And filled the beds of big-breasted bitches,
Covering them in quilts of fantasies
To blind his wicked eye which looked awry
On everything to concoct beauties
Only to buy and bend and bomb
So that the dance lasts on his soul's tomb.

Now old, bent, and wanting nothing
But his undoing, he builds edifices of poetic ruin,
Made out of his raging and rambling way of living,

To shout his pain out loud imagining
That the air, one winter evening,
Will carry his willful heart somewhere
Near his long-lost love's ear and take her back
All the way to the day she disarranged their zodiac.

Why I Never Told You

Do you know why I never
Told you that I loved to stare
At you hugging those paper
Bags down the old corridor?

Because such jiffs of pleasure
Should be untouched by chatter
And left alone in order
To continue to appear
Through my soul's narrow louvre;

So that you stay forever
Hugging those ravished paper
Bags down the old corridor,
All the way quite unaware
That this happens to structure
The whole world for a lover.

The Connection

Alright, so you ask me
What the connection is
Between wine and poetry.
Let me try to tell you:
Wine eliminates pretense;
It makes you face thoughts
Without the ideological sieve;
It puts you in contact with
Your beloved's flesh and juice
Without having to enact
The niceties and the tact;
It makes you go straight
To what is irking you without
Having to bother with side issues;
It gets to descriptive details
You can't possibly tolerate
When you are in a sober state;
It makes you love yourself
Enough to think that what
You need to say is actually
Important for others to know –
Even if it is not;
It reduces hours of deep
Thinking seriously hindered
By lots of signs that try
To hold you back and reign you in;
It takes you where you don't
Usually go because of fear.
It may not reveal any truth,
But it makes you knock
On its door relentlessly,

Knowing that it won't open.
It does not end suffering life
Or people or unrequited love,
But it can make you enjoy
The suffering endlessly.
That is the connection
Between wine and poetry.

A Dream

They invited me to their party in the shed.
They said, that in the name of brotherhood,
And the same blood, that runs in our veins,
We must be partners in the love of God.

The wine jug went round the room
From mouth to mouth. The piece of bread
Rapidly disappeared in so many hands.
The fragrant smoke of the shisha filled
The lungs, and the tears welled up
In the eyes as telltales of the living dead
Circulated with amazing speed through the heads.

A woman came in, completely covered
In pitch-black from head to toe. She was accused
Of being just too sexy behind the shroud;
That the wise can see with their special
Spectacles of searing sagacity that
Her breasts are still proud – behind the shroud.

No defense was around, so, she was hanged
By the tits from the holy chandelier and stoned
To death amid the hallelujahs of the children.

Children! Nobody said that there will be
Any kids in the goddamn shed, I thought.
"Oh yes", someone cried to me over the heads
As if he had instant access to my mind,
"We brought the kids to educate them".

At the top of their voices, the children yelled:

"Long Live the Law!" as they recorded
The execution with their mobile phones.
Others were sticking their tongues out
To catch the dripping milk and the blood.

I said to myself: "this must be a dream",
But I didn't scream, and sit up in my bed
Until a sweet and soft voice whispered in my ear:
"It is what it is in the eyes of God".

Sandy Eyes

I was just waiting for my mother
To pick me up after school,
Looking at nothing, thinking about nothing
But her arrival, when particles of sand
Flew out of this boy's hand
Like tiny bullets to fill my eyes,
Inflaming and blinding them for a few
But unusually long minutes.
There was no reason for that.

Years later, I was just trying to understand
The world through reading literature,
When those eyes with the colour of the sand
Blinded me again – this time,
For unusually long years to come.
There was no reason for that either.

Now, it is the memory of the sandy eyes –
Mine and yours – that dictates these lines
With a passion and a pain streaming through.
Sandy Eyes – the eyes still haunting me –
You might be surprised to know,
That the one thing I ever wanted to do
Is to see my eyes looking at you.

The Smile

The physical body, my good friends, never lies;
It acts, every time, and tells the stark truth in full,
Even when it doesn't want to be so truthful,
Even when the truth tortures it beyond pleasure,
Even when it must confess all its juices out
Like a sinner who can't help but sin and repent.

Guarding integrity till it withers and dies,
The body can't be but freewheeling to the end,
Yet, as there must be one tiny traitor at least
In every land, system, family or country,
The body, too, must have its own double-dealer –
A nice subtle site for accommodating fakeness;

The face is its unique place of frank phoniness.
To be honest with you, this is why I oft felt
That I did understand every single movement
Of those titillating twisting tasty bodies,
But it is also why I wrote for thirty years
To deal with the charming but equally false smile –

Why I drink to smile as someone else for a while.

A Better Moslem

Well, I know how to pretend;
I've been pretending all my life,
I still do.
Pretending is the easiest thing to do,
So, if you'd like me to act
As if I do not know you,
Let us do this little skin show.
I guess, for us, it shouldn't be a problem.

However, my dear old friend
From the days of hunger and strife,
Look at you!
Frowning over nowt with this beard that you grew
For style, image or impact,
But why should it make you throw
A friendship out of the window
Thinking you're now, somehow, a better Moslem?

She Actually Left

This time,
She actually left.
I thought it would be less painful,
Since I ran that scenario
Several times
Through my head.

For I also wished,
Many a time,
To have all the time
For myself again,
And my writing,
And my wine.

Who needs a woman
To be able to write poetry?
No one.
People impede creativity –
They should be banned
From my vicinity.

***

This is the seventh night –
Without a single scribble.
This … pen …
Is in such a sorry condition.
This … pen …
Is somehow sluggish.

***

Damn!

One-dimensional Man: Remembering D. H. Lawrence

When we first met,
It was like one-dimensional man
Meeting one-dimensional woman;
Blood knowledge hid behind our shut eyes.
We weren't able yet
To see ourselves eating the forbidden fruit.
Our blood and red wine were one.
We simply basked in divine light.
We had no use for eyesight,
As we were one-dimensional figures on God's slate.
We were ignorant but not stupid,
And our ignorance underpinned
Our erotic existence,
Brimming over the top of the holy cup
Of pure pleasure as worship –
We and the world were one.

And because our souls were naked,
We didn't see the nakedness of our bodies –
It didn't matter to us
What is naked enough
To make any meaning.
We were happy and meaningless
In transitions that didn't need translations.
The energy of the powerful poetry penned
Down on God's slate
By our teetering dance
Of the tarantula tore apart
Everything that didn't belong to our sexual song.

Now, that we became three-dimensional beings
Over the years,
Everything that matters is lost.
We see more, we know more,
We can even draw portraits of ourselves.
We can reflect on our nakedness.
And I can write this poem.
And you can read it.
But "the more we know,
The less we are",
As Lawrence once said.

A Caring but Perverse Poet

It's 2022 now,
Or 1984, well,
It doesn't matter,
As long as you'll let me tell you
About George Orwell.

You must be surveilled,
Your every movement must be monitored.
Most important of all,
Your ears have to be open.
You must be ready all the time
To sacrifice yourself
Even when innocent of any crime,
Especially when innocent of any crime.

You see? If you're not ready to be
Falsely accused of anything out of the blue,
That is the ultimate guilt
And the unforgivable sin.
You must be veiled, too,
And shut out, and shut up.
And, by the way,
So that you do not misunderstand,
And become a loving slave,
Let me make myself clear;
I don't want your love,
Never really wanted it;
I only want your respect.

See how humble I am?
I don't want to cost you much.
So, read my words and surrender
All your orifices, but not your heart.
That's all you have to do.
The gapes, the holes – no exception.
Isn't it better than selling your soul
To the devil that people call
Love for want of a better word
For good old human deception?

The Unsaid

Yesterday,
The best of all moments
Was when her face appeared at the door,
When her body occupied that space in the room,
And when her voice filled the air.

Today,
The memory of that moment
Feels like being on a galloping horse,
Quivering violently over the quivering ground,
Losing balance and the reins.

Now,
He has learnt something new;
Just as her riveting appearance
Always prophesied her disappearance,
The unsaid is not unsaid.

Exams

Someday, some people will have to do something
About the systems of education in some societies.
For when you keep having a recurring nightmare
Till the age of fifty, when your head is mostly white hair,
About not being adequately prepared
For a school exam tomorrow morning

And wake up in the middle of the night out of terror
Only to thank heavens it was just a bad dream,
There must be something wrong with your upbringing
By a system that seems to have made sure
To traumatize your childhood and that this trauma
Will be reconstituted endlessly in the future.

I am fifty-two;
Those dreams stopped two years ago –
Not without a trace though,
Because I still get a certain pang in the stomach
When one of my children tells me
They have an exam tomorrow.

Green Bottle

Hey green bottle
Of Gold Medal
Taiwan Beer!
I did not come here
To just watch you
And empty your
Numbing content;
I came to write,
And, you're supposed to help.

What are you doing here
Distinctive Flavor Lager Beer?
This can't be why you got
Your Gold Medal –
It's not about your sight;
It should be about the insight
You're supposed to bring forth.
Don't tell me I'm gonna pay this bill
Just for the nice taste and the chill.
If there's nothing to tell,
Then this has been
A waste of time,
Green bottle with the Gold Medal.

Oh, I see it now –
So, this was about you;
You decided to talk about
Yourself today;
You abandoned your sense
Of service and sacrifice;
You decided to be selfish

For a change.
Yet in your selfishness,
You're still giving me something here,
Unbelievably generous beer!

Memory

Open spaces
Always remind me of young love;
The expanse of the sea
And the strong smell of iodine;
The mountains of Hong Kong;
The tortuous Chinese gardens,
And the tree trunks that we coiled up around.

God misplaces
A man's mature mind far enough
From the wildness of youth
And the rush of adrenaline –
Lest memory gets hung
On fumbling feminine fens
While bodies disappear in their surround.

Sinai

In the desert of Sinai,
The stars seemed to be closer.
The cold night, though quiet,
Had the loudest voice.
The mountains made me feel
Insignificant.

The Bedouins smoked
Like there was no tomorrow.
European tourists sat around the fire,
Listening to my stories with
Sleepless eyes spelling desire –
For the sand spoke of horses and blood
And deities made of mud
That drove numberless armies through the desert
With an eye on beautiful Kemet.

I used to think of one thing; how to bring
The stars down to earth.
They "do not give a damn", as Auden said,
Yet, they did look down upon me that night
And assured me that one day I will write
About them from a foreign land,
When they become one with the one
Who broke my heart, back in Cairo,
And released the ceaseless ink of this pen.

Haters and Lovers

Who said that hatred has to be a horrid thing?
Coming to think about those moments of the spring
Of negative energy and the spiky looks

In the eyes of the malicious, I can't but link
Loving the lonely state of mind and the fine drink
That drove frenzied poetic words – psyche to ink –

With those who kept their antagonistic distance
To avoid the incomprehensible distress
Connected with being in my vicinity.

Antithetically, those who gave everything
Out of tough love, and thus could do nothing but cling
To the boring intellectual and his books,

Despite how often he did drive them to the brink
Of sanity with his mind going out of sync
Fitfully, not knowing the straight line from the kink,

Couldn't avoid being a constant disturbance –
A changeless bliss, which nevertheless must oppress
Dear loneliness and its twin – creativity.

A Confession of Love

Seeing her face,
After thirty years
Of longing and loss,
He decided to confess,
And tell her about all
The little big things he missed.

They settled down,
He ordered the wine,
Took a long deep breath
And said: "I have to piss".

As the stream hit the bowl,
Relieving him of his heavy load,
He started talking to the wall.

"I always felt that something
Remained forever undone;
I should've danced with you
That night on a candle light.
I should've photographed you reading
Lady Chatterley's Lover in bed.
I should've paid more attention
To the lips I took for granted back then.
I should've sketched those fingers
Before the onslaught of wrinkles.
I should've listened to your complaints
With an open heart.
I should've stayed longer hugging you
From behind while you pretended
To describe the mosque's steeple

And talk about the tiny people
Walking the streets below.
I wonder who we are now though".

The stream has stopped long time ago.
He was still facing the wall,
Trying his best to understand,
With his tool of expression in his hand.

When he returned to the table,
She was waiting in anticipation.
But he had nothing more to say to her;
The confession was made
To the wall with the hole
That took all of his piss
Silently without getting bored
With his sad story.

The Voices

There is something beyond beauty,
Touching the soul and the body,
About the voices
Of readers pouring poetry
Into my ears.

In terms of material gain,
There's nothing to obtain
From this seemingly
Ungainly activity
For any of us.

Why do we keep
Reading those words?
Why never do we
Get tired of listening
To the voices?

If spending precious time
Is about making choices,
Then there must be
Something at play
Beyond pleasure and happiness
In this almost numbing
Reciting of bizarre
Linguistic experiences
And listening to them.

It is not okay;
There are certain people
Walking this earth

Like everybody else,
But not exactly communicating
Like everybody else.

I believe that the messages
They pass mouth to ear
With the physicality
Of their vocal cords
Unsettle whole worlds,
Destroy enemies, far and near,
Inundate landscapes
With fluids of the body,
And impose a dictatorship
Upon the land –

For what is one poetic voice
But one view, one style
Penetrating the whole universe,
In volatile verse,
And whatever the king says
Goes?

Blanchot

I didn't know
Back in 2008
That one day I will be arrested
By the memory of her
Discussing Blanchot,
Whom I never cared to teach.
How did that image from the past
Catch up with me?
The boring conference,
The intellectual circus
At The Westin Long Beach –

Four days of quest in the ultimate West,
Yet, on the third,
We had to sneak out;
The beautiful philosophy PhD
Bewitched me – still a candidate
Back than at HKU's Complit.
We took the train to Los Angeles
Just to see
The HOLLYWOOD sign on Mount Lee
And witness the decadence
Of the Avenue of the Stars.

Back to The Westin at night,
To make sure the egotistic show
Was over, but then Blanchot
Made an entrée,
Son of a b …, and he
Made her dive too deep in philosophie
Française

That turned red wine into café au lait,
Just beside the bed
But not on it,
Till the rooster crowed at dawn.

It wasn't how I planned my trip
To the US of A –
The end of the world.
I don't understand though
Why it still feels so painful
To remember and think
How I had to depart with Blanchot
And return to Hong Kong –
O, responsabilité!

Hong Kong Social Distancing

The bartender announces
It is now 06:00 p.m.
Everyone should leave.
A few unsuspecting souls
Pay the bill
And rush out of the door.
Those who know HK well
Stay though –
They order more drinks.
The assistants roll down
And turn off the lights
As pints and half-pints
Go round as usual
Till dawn.

The ever-flickering lights
Of massage parlors
Are out now all the time.
Those places look dark
Through the windows
Just the same.
Novices do not know
Much about the game.
Experienced customers
Know it's just a show.
In room 5, in the dark,
A man suffers silently
While a fat woman
Smilingly twists his little toes.
In room 6, another is having sex
With a professional prostitute
Pretending to be a masseuse.

Incredible

The presenter didn't seem to believe
What she was presenting.
She talked about the 'Incredible people"
She met on the internet;

The 'incredible filmmaker'
Who made a short feminist film
About women's participation
In the country's political realm;

The 'incredible artist'
Who designed a hall of fame
Filled with photographs
Of great women in Arab history;

The 'incredible businesswoman'
Who inherited a fortune
From her father and is now
Bossing an army of fathers around.

And, of course, the 'incredible Sheikh'
From the oil-rich country
Who happily financed all of this
Incredibility.

I couldn't but notice
The incredible number of times
She had to pull forward her head cover –
Which kept sliding back while she talked –
Revealing a lock of her frontal hair;

A gesture which somehow
Timed itself perfectly
With the utterance
Of the word 'incredible'.

In the detailed questionnaire
Sent afterwards to the audience,
I skipped everything and answered
Only the last question;

'Overall, what do you think
About the presentation?'
I wrote down one word:
Incredible.

The End of the Road and the Roma Rosso

I think I've reached
The end of the road –
Finally.
There's nothing left
Except to do my job,
Blindly,
Write as much as I can
For some reason
I fail to understand,
And make love,
Occasionally.

How strange to remember
The days of competition.
What was that all about?
And how did past foes
Become best friends?
How did some kinships
Turn into true enmities?
And how did the girl I loved
In my youth become this
Intolerable woman?

Unfortunately,
Or rather fortunately,
Italian wine
Only poses questions;
It never gives answers.

No Narrative

There is no narrative here, my love.
The past is anything but mythical,
And I have no regrets about lost youth.
The truth is that those magnificent

Legs and arms reiterate beyond doubt
That enjoying life has no story to tell
Or to be written in any form anywhere.
Life, in here, does not progress,

And its ultimate pleasures just come,
And when they go, they go for good;
Nothing can come in their stead,
Yet, other pleasures always appear

With different smiling faces.
These ones are not replacements,
For there is also no substitution –
There's nothing but metamorphoses.

A Feminist Bride

Before you make love to me,
Let me cut off your penis;
Let's start on a ground of equality.
I make the rules now,
Within academia and without,
And you're out.

You must be queer, or,
If you don't like it
And would rather keep your
Holes whole and intact,
At least you should've the tact
Of letting me lead you through this.

Don't you want to be healthy?
Aren't you drinking beer without
Alcohol and coffee without caffeine?
Smoking cigarettes without nicotine?
Why shouldn't you make love to me
Without your precious penis?

Find a way! You always did;
You wanted to be here;
You've been seeking purity;
You loved playing with abstraction.
Don't tell me you'll back out now!
It is just too late for both of us.

This has gone beyond trend and fashion;
It has become a passion.
So, man up and try to suppress
The scream of your castration!

Unforgiven

They taught us at school
To forgive, but not to forget;
They told us that this is how
Civilization has evolved.
Forgive! So that you can
Maintain ethical authority.
Don't forget! Make sure to get
Your accounts straight.

I look at your eyes over
This cup of Turkish coffee
And say: What a crock of shit!
What does it mean to have
All the traits of virility
In your eyes and yet
Not become the father
Of your children?

What does it mean to have
All your love and respect
But not your body?
Who has the right to have it then?
Moses? Jesus? Mohammed?
Almighty God in heaven?
Forgive my incivility, but,
I am just another sinner,
And you will remain forever
Unforgiven.

Let Them Come

I say,
Let them come and save me
From my impulsiveness,
Let them come and save me
From red wine and writing,
From desperation,
Failure,
Lost love,
Unrequited love –
Let them come and save my soul
Because while saving it,
They'll have to deal with the body too,
They'll have to exorcise
The devil of poesy
And free me
From my haunting
Ghosts and illusions –
Let them drug my body
To cure my soul,
If they think that the soul
Can be cured in the first place.
What do I care?
I am not Joseph,
I don't want to be,
I'm just a sinner who
Wants to be saved,
And nothing can save a sinner
From the sin of writing
Other than the sin of falling
In love for no good reason
But to fall in the trap

God intended for man
To ease his earthly pain.

Ego and Body

The ego is that big devil
That makes you lose some people.
It's not bad at all for writing,
But it's terrible for your body.
For the body quite simply
Needs other people
To be able to be aware
Of its solitary existence.

In ancient Egypt and Babel,
The monks did know the worth of people;
Inside temples, they jailed writing,
And liberated the rude body –
Made it continually
Open to people –
Always in their desires' snare,
Taking care of its own subsistence.

An Egyptian Majnoon

There are those who prefer to stay safe
Inside their cultural cocoon,
And those who venture outside
To see what's different about
The idolized inside.
Consider me an Egyptian majnoon,
But I do think that if you decide
To leave your comfort zone
And unsettle your own mind,
At least do it with style.
It has become utterly cheap
To cry and cling to roots
And be sad and melancholic
And in-between and alcoholic
So that the world around you
Believes that you're different.
Style isn't about difference;
It's about entering a crowded room
And leaving after a few drinks
Without gazing at anyone –
And without being noticed by anyone.
That's when you're part of the environment.
That's also when you can be interesting,
By chance, to someone, or, to anyone.
Love doesn't come to the different.
It may come to the indifferent.

The Encounter on the Bridge

I should've smiled on that bridge
Where I passed by my death
And saw the fatal face
For the last time.
I should've smiled –
Out of courtesy.
It is not – that I cannot –
Go back in time
That irks me;
It is the lack of courage –
The inability to control my breath
And the contortions of my face
Facing the fatal face.
I should've smiled on that bridge –
And it is not the irreversible
That dictates
This melancholy –
It is the little dark,
The irreducible
Mark
That the brief encounter
Has left in me –
Forever.

Saxophone

Do you remember the repetitive
Musical sentence of the saxophone
That evening when we sat alone
In Carnegies close to Christmas 1996?
You said "this is going to be our tone
Tonight – let us also borrow the tempo".

The game of analysis we played that night
Remained so vivid in my mind
That seeing you now – all inhibited and timid –
Makes me wonder if you're the same woman.

What happened to the sax and the sex
And the Egyptian-German-Indian mix
Of a woman who wasn't worried
About the demon underneath her skin?

To be honest, you scared me back then
When you so sensitively spoke
About the shape of the saxophone,
And how it seemed to invoke

In you a sense of innovation,
A desire for dangerous exploration –
You scared me to the point of
Disappearance in pleasure.

Since when you've been hiding
Yourself under that cover?
When did you decide to be dead
In the eyes of formerly "little" men?

When did you decide to damage the image
Of woman and the world and God?

Tucking Status Quo

"God does not change a people's condition
Unless they themselves change their condition" –
Qur'anic Sura Alra'ad, Verse one-one.

So, when a system tells you that if you have nothing,
You should simply go tuck yourself
Because no one would be willing
To tuck you, asshole,
You shouldn't be surprised;
You're not economically viable,
Which means that no one
Would be interested in you –
Not even losers like yourself.

In this bonanza, losers crush losers;
They can openly be the worst tyrants.
And when one underdog is elected
For a seat of power by other underdogs,
Guess what? the first thing he usually does
Is to betray and oppress his own blood
In the great Name of the Father – Amen!

The rich tucks the poor, the poor tucks the poor,
The voiceless the voiceless, the dumb the dumb,
The black the black, the women the women,
The hindered exotic the exotic.
It's just like that, quite homoerotic,
Ask Spivak; she would say that you can't speak.
And God seems to approve this arrangement
Because everyone is happy with it.
I mean, why expect a change from above
When you are clearly enjoying yourself?

New Attendant

You'll have to excuse them,
My dear;
These white-haired men are full of wine
And beer.
They are also full of memories –
Many memories
Of successes and failures with women,
As well as too many faces
To distinguish which belongs to whom,
And, they're just too drunk
To mind the difference
Between the bar and the bedroom.

At this age, it doesn't really matter
Any more
When you're drunk and old and bald.
I am old and bald,
But not drunk yet.
You can still converse with me
Without having to worry
About my hands –
They're busy anyway,
You see?
Writing sensuality
Instead of acting upon it.

Too elitist for you?
Okay,
Wait until I am drunk too,
Then you'll see
This man of letters can be

The worst love hound of desire
From the depth of Hellfire.

An Advice to Islamists

I woke up one day
To this euphoria
Everywhere
Inside the public toilet
We call 'social media'.
"He's dead! He's dead!",
Everyone was yelling
As if they were truly oppressed
By some powerful tyrant
Who's now finally dead.

I checked –

Only to discover
The celebrations are held
Because one thinker
Left this world
At the age of seventy-four
After writing eleven books
On Islamic terror –
Something just too present
To be denied.

I could've understood
The schadenfreude
If they were able to
Have the man destroyed
Before disseminating
What they see
As his incriminating
Dangerous philosophy.

But what does it mean
To be happy because someone
You couldn't debate with
Is now dead?
What else can provide
A stronger proof
That you
And the culture you belong to
Are just too scared
Of one free mind?

If your whole world
Collapses because one man
Happens to differ,
Then maybe you should
Start to wonder
If you are blind.

Poetry between the Sheets

One of the greatest lessons
Of this strange life of alienation
In such an alienating city
Is an intellectual conversation
Between the crisp sheets
While the national anthem plays
To the romance of her body.

That particular one was a continuation
Of a discussion on writing poetry.
What is the worth of this submission
To others who wouldn't care
About one's personal fantasy?
It's not about others, we concluded,
But the persistent actualization
Of a life beyond this dreary reality.

For this murky morass of banality
Surrounding us is not enough
To make us real, and between
The sip of red wine and the kiss,
Our mortal bodies can only live on
As a recurring image in poetry.

Lost Cause

In defense of my lost cause,
I would say that as you should be the enemy of culture,
According to Freud,
My dear deer of the dry desert of Egypt,
I must've been nothing but a vulture
That wanted to draw lines of blood
On your behind with its claws.

Of course, you were absolutely right.
The proof is that I eventually became a stern scholar
Of comparative literature.

You can't blame a bird of prey.
Do you see it now? You do not belong enough to nature.
I believe Freud's wrong;
You are family, you are civility and stability.
It is in fact I who belong to the savage Sahara.
I took Freud and Marx and Nietzsche
Down the course of my lost cause,

Across my dry desert forever.
For behind every beautiful woman in literature,
There must be a pervert writer.

Authenticity

What do you mean you wanted
Authentic words of love?
The poem I handed
To you with shaking hands,
Written by Aboul-Qacem Echebbi
Was authentic enough –
For love.

Well, yes, I know, the words were
Not written by me,
But what does this have to do with
Authenticity?

Don't you know that Echebbi
Words attach to feelings that match
With this inexplicable inundation
That must be kept under lock and key
And latch lest the guards of the jealous
God of the tighteous good grind us
For blasphemous food before I can
Even think of words to put on paper
That cannot in any case be
But borrowed from books and bards
And banks of the surrogate
So that I can never get
To put my hands on the flanks
I've been dreaming of
For a thousand and one nights?

What can neither be detached
Or reattached is that touch of the palm
That passed between us
When I handed you the poem –
That sexual intercourse,
You know,
Which never took place.

Being a Poet

You don't have to be a poet
To be a poet.
When your writing touches
A sensitive chord,
You're a poet.
When it is poignant enough
To make them think,
You're a poet.
When they don't know
Whether to laugh or cry,
You're a poet.
When you think too much
Yet think that you don't
Think at all,
You're a poet.
When writing becomes
More enjoyable
Than being with a beautiful
Woman in bed,
You're definitely a poet.
When you read in the morning
What you wrote last night
And think it doesn't make sense,
You're a poet.
When you make unthinkable
Efforts just to avoid
Being with people,
You're a poet.
When you think
That the people you love
Impede writing a poem

More than inspire it,
You're a poet.
When you think solitude
Is poetry,
You're a poet.
When you think God
Is a poet,
You're a poet.

Threatened to Be Left Alone

Please don't make
That particular mistake.
My happiness does not
Depend on you,
Or on any other woman.
I am not scared
Of being left alone
With this pen and paper;
You'll have to cease being narcissistic.

You can't shake
Or unmake this primal ache
Which, earlier, did not
Depend on you,
Sweet but arrogant woman.
I'm indebted
For being left alone
With this pen and paper;
And, yes, this poetry is onanistic.

Surreal

It was surreal
To see her again
After so many years;
So many ups and downs,
More downs than ups,
So many failures,
So many rejections,
Unpublished essays,
Unpublished poems,
Fake job interviews,
Financial bottlenecks,
So many faces
Of people I couldn't stand,
And so many other women
Who were different
Yet the same.

She took a deep breath and said:
"I just wanted to say
That I never forgot the way
You made love to me".

It felt good to know
That there was actually
One thing that I did right –
Unequivocally.

Half-circle Balconies

Sometimes,
A man cannot explain
Why certain sights
Seem to be sexiest.
Every time,
I pass by the building
With the half-circle balconies,
I stand for a while –
Staring at it in awe.
The architect
Must be a genius.
The white balconies
Protrude perfectly
From the building's body,
Each with a brown blot
In the middle of the curve.
The overhang effect
Seems to be felt
Even from afar.
I see myself hanging dangerously
From one of those half-circles
By the lips –
Against the law of physics.
Why do I love those balconies so much?
Because I never had a balcony in Hong Kong?
Or because this balcony
Seems to speak to my psyche
About certain aesthetics?

The Impossible Woman

If you meet the impossible woman who
Doesn't exist, let her know that every word
Here was written because of her and for her.

Let her know that every nipple I touched made
Its distinct presence through her untouched nipples.
Let her know that every little sip of wine
Was made to be erotic only because
The glass, to me, was always her parting lips,
And that I only drank for the sole purpose
Of making her features exist on paper.

Let her know that if beautiful Myrrha
Didn't seduce her old father in the dark,
We wouldn't have the tender shade of the tree
In the northern deserts of black Africa,
Nor the medicine for colds, cough or asthma.
Let her know that Zeus, the swan, raped Leda
On that armchair only for good literature.

So, if you do meet her walking barefooted
On the burning sands of the ancient desert,
Let her know, she, will always be, chased by me;
That she will ever be sought, dead or alive.
Let her know she's this pen's ink, this body's life.
Let her know that her seduction created
Both the fire of desire and smart art.

Let her know that she has always been, and will
Ever be, the vast Sahara in my heart.

Dangerous Liquid

The gin made different cigarettes
Taste the same.
Her brush strokes were
Indecipherable to me,
Yet, I could feel each
Like a slap on my face.
Sound contrasted with color
To such an extent
That I felt
Like licking all the paint
Clean off the slate.

She wasn't painting,
I thought,
But torturing
An imaginary being.
Was it herself?
I wondered,
Trying to play the philosopher
As usual.
The violent hand moves
Didn't give me time
To finish a thought;
They Caught
The vibrations of determined arms
And other charms
And legs like two anchors
On the floor.

The gin, the cigarettes,
The words, the colors,

And the bits of flesh
Concocted a language
In the eyes;
Somehow, we both felt
Like performing some dangerous feat;
Somehow, we both thought
We will still end up on our feet;
Without falling in love;
Without weakness;
Without reifying art.

It was such a bad idea to think
We could get away with it.
The face which suddenly appeared
On the slate
Seemed to reiterate:
"You do not mess
With the color-less
Drink!

Counterfeit Money

If you consider this counterfeit money
Passed from hand to hand unimportant,
Then you are greatly mistaken.
For people do need to see false smiles
And words coated in honey
Even when they know they are.
They are not meant to be taken
For true my chillingly rational avatar.
They're only meant to be used as reasons
To go on with the façade.
After all, it is the only
Mode of being allowed to anyone.
If you haven't heard, or, if you weren't
Able to get over Hemingway,
Then I am sorry to say
That I have to try to tear you away
From the honesty of Hemingway.
This is not an act of generosity,
And I am not doing it for you.
If you have to take away
Everything you gave to me,
Please do it gently.
I will take your counterfeit money.

A Drunken Discourse of Love

Under the spell of wine, the world
Becomes strangely tolerable,
And I see in you much more than you;
I see beauty without knowing where
It comes from or what it acts on.
The repetitive and senseless music
That is playing becomes Beethoven.
The bog of reality surrounding us
Magically becomes a sort of heaven.
Insignificant details become significant –
Like the little dark spot on your chin.
And I seem to capture the veneration
Of things before they disappear,
And I seem to understand in time,
For a change, not after suffering loss.
And God, somehow, seems to be
On our side, loving our weaknesses.
And He seems to be helping me
To pour those words into your ear.
And the discourse of love, written
Like verse in your eyes and on your skin,
Is sung by the universe through the sky
All the way up to invisible Eden.
So, in essence, we shouldn't forget
The presence of the good old red aqua –
Our great companion in this ménage à trois.

Recurring Dream

'This time', I told myself,
'I am going to face them no matter what'.
I didn't enter any of the buildings
As I usually do to avoid being shot;
I stood still in the middle of the lane.
People ran past me screaming,
As the bangs got louder.
I began to tremble,
But I didn't want to hide like every time.
I get shot every time anyway.

Somehow, they always manage
To spot me watching the carnage
From my hiding place –
A moment wholly hideous –
And the bullet, always,
Arrives at its destination.
I was determined
To look my shooter in the eye for a change.
I could now hear
The armors approaching loud and clear.

'This is the moment of truth', I thought,
'Get a grip for once and get shot
Standing in the middle of the lane!'
I knew there must have been
A thousand eyes watching me from hideouts.
'What is this fool doing?',
I heard someone whispering,
'Doesn't he know he's going to ruin the show?'
I have to admit
I didn't understand that bit.

As the fearsome armor
Made a halt a few feet in front
Of my shaking body, a surprised soldier
Emerged from the hatch on its turret.
'So, you finally got it!', he said smilingly,
'Good bye and good luck!'
The recurring dream of almost five years
Never came back.
But since I'm now writing this poem,
I must assume that I do miss it.

She Knows

She knows
I'm burning all of those paper boats
Out of despair.
She knows
That all my quarrels
With my foes
And the merciless words
I stab them with
Are nothing but throws
Around her body –

She knows
That the religious debate
With those airheads
Is a show of hate –
Displaced –
Around the young heart
That she ate.

She knows
That the golden hair
She shielded and showed
At will –
In spite of the sheikhs'
Ridiculous hold
On the secret keys
Of heaven and hell –

Weakens my knees
As I go on raising my sword
Up in the air
And darting it down
Upon the necks
Of the demure –

Those who cannot
See the connection
Between the divine
And the ruthless sadism
Of a beloved woman.

Inspired by "because i am a sled dog"
By Poet Laureate of the Yukon, PJ Yukon

Two Ladies with Two Dogs

Two ladies
With two dogs
Meet in the middle of the street.
One lady talks about her late husband
And how good he was –
Too good to be her husband.

The other talks about her living spouse
And what a cheat he is,
And how he always tries to arouse
Other women's interest in him.
And the problem is
They usually respond –
The bitches.

The two ladies keep discussing,
Laughing, and putting the blame
On Mame.
Meanwhile,
The two dogs are sniffing
Each other's derrières
Without any sense of guilt –
Without any shame.

Someday,
Someone should explain
Why some have the right to talk
While others are muzzled
And tied with a chain.

Your Silent House

I always
Wanted to enter
Your silent house –
To gently open its gate
With my trembling hands,
Hearing my pounding heart,
As I go in and roam around
Gazing for a long time at
The pictures of the dead
Hanging on the wall,
And touch your teenage bed
With my sinful fingers
As a pervert sheikh
With a long beard
Who prays and masturbates
In the same holy spot,
And loves God –
Because it is convenient.
It's cold outside.
Creative,
But cold.

Fragmentary View

I am not very selective
When I am drunk,
You see,
Your ugliness
Can actually work
After being broken down
Into little detailed beauties
By this miraculous liquid,
So, don't waste the chance
Of this fragmentary view,
And please leave
Before I get sober again.

Sobriety is not
Very humanistic;
We become humane,
According to our own
Written definitions,
Only when we drink.
Generosity is not
Very compatible
With being sober
And only human –
It has to be drawn
By the devil's work.

Most of the time though,
We are with God,
And He is a great artist;
He has no taste
Or tolerance

For those
Who are not perfect –
Like himself.
We create beauty
To be little gods,
Yet, right now,
Even beauty's a defect.

Assessment

If I am to assess
Those 12 years of a relationship
Based on your lovely behind,
I'd be at a total loss;
That one body part
Can actually obsess
Someone's imagination
For such a long time
Seems fictional.

Excuse me, Miss,
But I also have to confess
That besides adoring your backside,
Some writing was done aside,
On the margins of the derriere,
And I have to say
That the beautiful prat
Taught me things I wasn't good at.

I learnt how to appreciate
Imperfect shapes
And unusual landscapes –
I learnt that beauty
Has no definition
And art cannot be
A word in a dictionary;
It is just like your haunches –
It plays with imagination
Until it launches
Its full-fledged attack
On sexuality,

On the marker of humanity,
On the world itself,
And on poetry.

Black

In the name of ethics,
And Betjeman's "Senex",
Forbid black, the color of death,
From becoming
The Color of underwear.

Forbid it too from becoming
The color of hair.

Why do you think the black flag of cholera
Was raised by old Ariza
On the ship where
He made long due love to Daza?
For keeping away people
From a vessel
Infected with passion for Fermina?

The flag, because it was black,
Detonated danger,
And not just the danger of disease or death –
But the danger of the color of death,
Which was, for sure,
The color of Daza's suspenders.

Black is not for pretenders;
It doesn't reflect anything
But the might of absorption,
And before you realize being
In the realm of death,
You'd come face to face with the flesh,
And dive where the self disappears,

Every time, with no exception,
Yet comes out of darkness claiming
That it was alive and kicking.
What deception!

Poetic Messages

Well, all those coded messages
That we seem to send all the time
To each other in poetry
Aren't getting us anywhere,
While our big heads are getting
Wiser and whiter, day and night.

Woman, that's enough messages!
Don't you think it is about time
We put aside dear poetry
And try to start heading somewhere
South far from the heads and letting
The bodies talk instead all night?

The Onslaught of Sameness

"And there came dreadful sameness
My long-lost lonely lover.
I'm sorry it took me some
Time to write you this letter.

Let me say that I never
Doubted your heart or your love;
I never imagined that
Anyone would love me more,
But, by the time your muse came
To understand the meaning
Of your young uniqueness,
The depth of penetration
That accompanies your name,
Everything became the same.

People's faces mingled and
Became one big listless face,
The trees around our old place
That we named one by one in
Our dreamy youth became
Just local flora to my
Deteriorated eyesight.
The cats, somehow, lost their grace;
They obeyed now without shame.
The warm seasons lost passion,
And the winter lost its bite.

The "dog from hell" that you kept
Making up in your poems
To chase you all of your life
Didn't seem to be any
Different from the stray dogs the
Authorities killed around
This place every other night.

Yes, I have been thinking of
The loving look in their eyes –
Those dogs that resembled you –
And I did cry once or twice
When I remembered their barks –
And your words and your poems –
The rattling of chains inside
The van of the dog police;
The rattling of chains inside
Your wounded masochist heart –
That dog that you crucified
At my dead-end street and my
Small untouchable garden –
Untouchable just to you,
Simply because you were and
Still are too much to handle.

When sameness finally came,
It made my days, my nights, my
Cigarettes, my body parts
And everything all the same.
It is now for this reason
All my parts are united
In the thought that your dear love
Must remain unrequited".

Ms. Li Wants Me to Be Sober

Ho!
Beautiful Ms.,
Could there be anyone,
Anything, anywhere, anyhow,
In this whole wide world
That is important enough
For me
To be sober
To deal with?

The fact is
It's all over,
Ms. Li,
Trying to be soft or tough;
Look bored or ignored.
I love your lower lip and raised brow,
Yet, still stands the question,
So, the answer is
No.

The Future Is Already Here

The future is already here.
We all know it; we are not blind.
Look at the boats and the dead
Children on the shore.
Look at Brett Kavanaugh boofing
His way to the Supreme Court.
Look at Professor Ford giving
Him sensational publicity boofing
His way to the Supreme Court.
Look at the mesmerizing fear
In the eyes of passersby
If you sneeze – in your own mask.
Look at the Islamic beards
Taking back Kabul in no time,
Putting millions of women back
In the dark in no time.
Will any of us be surprised or
Depressed if after a few years
Concentration camps reappear somewhere?
Aren't we already there?
The future is already here.
This is a fascist statement.
The future is already here,
And it is a fascist future.

Love and Fantasy

I usually give people
Another chance –
Never a tyrant
In my reactions,
Never seek revenge –
Not because I'm generous,
But because it takes too much
Work, energy, time –
It is just easier to forgive
And indulge again
In my own self –
Or my own selfishness.

I don't know why
I insisted to get back
That time, my love.
See? The only instance
In which I decided
To become less Self-centered
And make some connection
With someone else,
I lost you, squarely.

This proves I was right
All along
When I told you
That love isn't really
About anything between
Any two people;
It is about how good you are
At maintaining
Your own fantasy.

Drunk on a Bus

Well,
The lady
Who first sat beside me,
Opted to move, I guessed,
Because of the smell
Of alcohol
That filled
The atmosphere.

Hell,
She was dead right;
That was a dangerous
Territory –
Full of wild words,
Mixed with red wine,
Washed down
With dry beer.

So,
A beautiful reindeer,
Like the runaway Miss,
Should stay away
From this human mess
And continue to dream
About sweet love
And life and Christmas.

Your Rationality

Your rationality,
And authoritarian personality,
Worked quite well back then;
When I was too green
To intervene in my heart's desire.

Today, severity
Of old age and the sheer magnanimity
Of life's white hair rain
Stand firm in between
My heart and this pen which doesn't tire.

Simple Equations

While being high
On the red drink,
I tend to think
One can either
Make sweet and slow love
Or use the ink;
Beyond the magic of
Straight Hard liquor
That makes cigarettes
Taste all the same,
Red wine seems to equate
Women's apertures
With new poems.

The God of Wine

This time,
Declared the god of wine,
There will be no savior;
This time,
No woman is going
To offer herself;
This time,
You are by yourself
And me –
Let's see
How tough you are;
Let's see
If you can live
Without love,
Without women;
If you can be
Alone with me
And this wild pen.
Are you strong enough
To live without love?
Are you man enough
To depart
From your manhood
And become
A cold loveless god?

To the Unattainable Woman

You never gave me yourself,
You never gave me your sex,
But you did give me the strange sensuality
Of the roaring – and quite boring –
Self-annihilating intellectual;
The slender hands holding cigarettes,
The cloud of smoke, the endless talk,
The hunger for words and flipping pages,
The hunting of birds and making cages,
The red wine that made people
Beautiful enough to love casually
And to forget over a cup of coffee.

Were you to surrender to my love,
My love – and I still rather that you don't –
The cigarettes would lose death –
Their ultimate attraction.
And hunger, for both love and words,
Would be lost in your flesh –
The unattainable flesh
That made the vast Sahara
Of thoughts and poems and "I"
And "Ana" and "Ngo" and "Ich".

Dumb Enough to Love

She takes a slow and sedulous journey
From my toe upwards, as if
This has been mandated by God,
And I am dumb enough to love
A woman who never heeded my love.

She tells me how she is utterly
In a kind of love
She can't begin to explain,
That her stomach seems to be in constant pain
In my presence – an ache her face can't conceal.
And I am dumb enough to love
A woman who gave me nothing
But a heart made of steel.

She takes her clothes off
In slow motion, dancing for me,
And hoping that I would, at least,
Write a poem about just that,
If I am too tired, or too drunk,
Or too old, or too cold
To make love to her.
And I am dumb enough to write
A hundred and nine poems
For a woman who showed me nothing
But a cold shoulder.

And I am dumb enough to pen my love,
Unrequited, on this paper.

And I am dumb enough to love
Just the words she inspired hereof.

Withering Away

I looked at that man
Drinking alone in the corner
And imagined it must have taken
Numberless glasses of wine
On an empty stomach
To be able to wear down
To the near skeleton he was.

There's a certain grace
In being so skinny at an old age.
How come he didn't accumulate
Fat over so many years?
How many cigarettes did he smoke?
How many women did he sleep with?
How many meals did he skip?

It's a feat not to eat in such a fat city,
And he's still drinking away that mortal body.
What do I care about him anyway
To ask so many questions?
I don't know, but I seem to have
This strange urge to go over to him
And whisper in his old ears:

"Drink more, old timer!
The war you waged against yourself
To wither away isn't meaningless;
If I am to assess the worth of men
And their success in what they do,
I would say that you fulfilled your duty,
And, you also did it so gracefully.

Recommended Readings

Auden, W. H. *Auden: Poems*. Selected by Edward Mendelson. New York: Penguin Random House, 1995.

Barthes, Roland. *Roland Barthes by Roland Barthes*. Translated by Richard Howard. Illustrated edition. New York: Hill and Wang, 2010.

Betjeman, John. *Collected Poems*. 1st ed. New York: Farrar, Straus & Giroux, 2006.

Blanchot, Maurice. *The Infinite Conversation*. Translated by Susan Hanson. 1st ed. Minneapolis, MN: University of Minnesota Press, 1992.

Bukowski, Charles. *The Pleasures of the Damned: Poems, 1951–1993*. Illustrated edition. New York: Ecco, 2008.

Caronni, Paola. *Uncharted Waters*. Hong Kong: Proverse Hong Kong, 2021.

Derrida, Jacques. *Given Time: Counterfeit Money*. Translated by Peggy Kamuf. 1st ed. Chicago: University of Chicago Press, 1992.

Dostoyevsky, Fyodor. *Notes from Underground*. Translated by Richard Pevear and Larissa Volokhonsky. Reprint, New York: Vintage, 1994.

Freud, Sigmund. *Civilization and Its Discontents*. Edited and Translated by James Strachey. Reprint, New York: Norton, 2010.

———. *The Interpretation of Dreams*. New York: Penguin Group, 1992.

Hemingway, Ernest. *The Complete Short Stories of Ernest Hemingway: The Finca Vigia Edition*. 3rd ed. New York: Scribner, 1998.

Lacan, Jacques. *Anxiety: The Seminar of Jacques Lacan, Book X*. Edited by Jacques-Alain Miller. Translated by A. R. Price. Book X edition. Cambridge: Polity, 2016.

———. *Encore: The Seminar of Jacques Lacan: On Feminine Sexuality, the Limits of Love and Knowledge, Book XX*. Edited by Jacques-Alain Miller. Translated by Bruce Fink. 1st ed. New York: Norton, 1999.

Lawrence, D. H. *Lady Chatterley's Lover*. New ed. Ware, Hertfordshire: Wordsworth Editions, 2005.

———. *Studies in Classic American Literature*. Reissue edition. London: Penguin Classics, 1990.

Márquez, Gabriel Garcia. *Love in the Time of Cholera*. Reprint, New York: Vintage, 2007.

RECOMMENDED READINGS

Orwell, George. *1984*. Kolkata: Signet Classic, 1961.

Spivak, Gayatri Chakravorty. *Can the Subaltern Speak?* Edited by Amber Husain and Mark Lewis. London: Afterall, 2021.

Žižek, Slavoj. *The Plague of Fantasies*. London: Verso, 1997.

www.ingramcontent.com/pod-product-compliance
Lightning Source LLC
Chambersburg PA
CBHW070826100426
42813CB00003B/510